CHANGE

(will do you good)

CHANGE

(will do you good)

poems by

Gail Rudd Entrekin

Poetic Matrix Press

ACKNOWLEDGEMENTS

Grateful acknowledgement is made to the following journals where these poems first appeared:

The Alembic, Big Muddy, Birmingham Poetry Review, Chautauqua Literary Journal, Facets, Freshwater, *The Fourth Quarter: Poems about Retirement and Beyond* (University of Iowa Press), The Grove Review, Imaginari, Lily Literary Review, Poetic Matrix, Poetry Flash, Poetry Motel, Poetry Now, Red Wheelbarrow, Reed Magazine, Rogue Scholars Press, Sacramento Guide to the Arts, Sierra Journal, *Sierra Songs & Descants: Poetry & Prose of the Sierra* (Hip Pocket Press, 2002), Visions-International, Wild Duck Review and *Year 2000 Anthology* (Northern California Center for the Arts).

"Twenty Minutes Ahead of the Fire" was nominated for the 2004 Pushcart Prize by The Grove Review.

"Justice" placed third in the 2005 National Writers Union contest judged by Maxine Kumin.

Cover Art *Chamber of Light* by Steve Solinsky.

Copyright 2005 by Gail Rudd Entrekin

ISBN: 0-9714003-4-2

All rights reserved. No part of this book may be used or reproduced in any manner whatsoever without written permission, except in the case of brief quotations embodied in critical articles or reviews.

Poetic Matrix Press
PO Box 1223 Madera, CA 93639
559.673.9402 ~ www.poeticmatrix.com

For Charles, who makes everything possible.

For their love and support and for making time for the sharing of our ongoing life stories, thanks to my kids Katy, Nate, Demian, Beth, Caleb, Jassamine, and Ben and my forever friends Ellie and Coral. For writing support, thanks to the members of both my writing groups; to Brett Hall Jones, and to Molly Fisk and her Poetry Boot Camp members. And a big thanks to John Peterson for selecting the book and making it happen.

Contents

What We Want

ORANGE / 15
SECRETS / 16
THE YOUNGER MAN / 17
TWENTY MINUTES AHEAD OF THE FIRE / 19
THE COMPLAINT OF NOAH'S WIFE / 20
THEORIES / 21
RED IRISES / 22
ASK ME / 23
GETTING DONE / 25
AUTUMN / 26
CLEARING THE LAND (MENOPAUSE) / 27
HOT FLASHES / 28
RANDOMNESS / 29
FOR GABRIEL CATALFO (1983-1999) / 30
THE RECITAL / 32
THE DOOR / 33
THE MOTHERS SPEAK: WHAT WE WANT / 34

Your Face

MIDLIFE / 39
BLUE WHALES / 40
YOU, YOU MEAN / 41
AFTER SNORKLING AT MOLOKINI CRATER / 42
BEING LEFT ALONE IN THE CENTER OF THINGS / 43
MAKING DINNER / 45
THINGS YOU NEVER THOUGHT YOU COULD DO / 46
SPANISH DANCER WITH DIABETES / 48
THE CONVERSATION / 49
THE LONG NIGHT / 50

THIS IS JUST TO SAY   /   53
NATE'S QUESTION   /   54
THE WRESTLING TOURNAMENT   /   56
ARE YOU MINE?   /   58
FOR NATE, WANTING DESPERATELY TO GROW   /   59
THE DANCE SHOW   /   61
THE JOURNEY   /   63
JUSTICE   /   64
THE LESSON   /   66
RIDING WITH BEN, 19   /   67
YOUR FACE   /   68

What the Mind Wants

AN AGING WOMAN   /   71
WAITING TO BE A GRANDMOTHER   /   73
OLIVIA FOR A MINUTE   /   74
BELLY   /   75
WAILING   /   76
LAGUNA BEACH   /   77
THE FIRST CREATURE   /   78
PRACTICE   /   79
A DYING PLANET   /   81
AT KONA   /   82
SNORING   /   84
WHAT THE MIND WANTS   /   85

CHANGE

(will do you good)

What We Want

In spite of the arch-enemy sorrow, one can remain alive long past the usual date of disintegration if one is unafraid of change, insatiable in intellectual curiosity, interested in big things, and happy in small ways.

Edith Wharton

ORANGE

        is adrenalin alert
not all-out panic like red, running down the path
with an earthquake opening up behind you
or up the beach with a tidal wave at your back
but the sound of a window breaking in another room
when you're alone in the house
or a child so burning hot she can't lift up
her head to tell you. Orange is
call someone and call the right someone
line your words up in the order they need
to understand, do not slip over
into the red area where no words
only small bursts of carbon dioxide
puff from your mouth, and the day may be lost
the intruder knife you where you stand
the child fall from bad to worse, go black.

Orange is a fire that needs careful tending
lest the whole forest leap up roaring. Keep
orange in a sealed Tupperware container. Keep
orange off drugs. Orange stands there telling lies,
about to bolt for the door. Study orange.
Recite it. Prepare for it. Never relax and forget
exactly where you saw orange last.

Secrets

There is no clear moment –
never the tell-tale blood on a sheet
or a car's back seat –
just sometimes they kiss so long and so deeply,
feeling each other's hot skin, that they almost
do it in the woods with branches in their backs
and cold mud slipping up through the layers
of last fall's oak leaves – and sometimes it is
inexplicably over and he is all business,
all clothing and guilt, while she sits back
in panting confusion, heated and shaking –
and sometimes only lips and fingers
and they learn mouths – and sometimes in cars
with a gear shift knob painfully beneath them
in the very dark he starts to enter her, pulls back in fear
and panic — and after months of this hot secret thing
they think of condoms – and slowly they admit
to themselves what they have done
and, finally, what they will be unable
to stop.

The Younger Man

I took for granted your longing for me,
that I was beautiful to you
and soft, my skin resilient, dappled, shiny,
the thing your hands hungered for
even in sleep – that holding my small body
between your palms made you large and strong
and entering me filled you with the power
of giving in, giving yourself over to me
and I knew it would always be so.

But now the wound: that as my body ages,
this vulnerable soft sack that holds me,
you have brought a new obsession to our bed,
our daily lives – a younger man
taut, hard-bodied, bony, so my cheek
mashed against his clavicle aches for your softness,
the hollow where I laid my face,
nuzzled your warm smooth neck,
not this thin sinew so unwelcoming
and yet, so healthy and so beautiful!

We both marvel at him in the mirror.
Timidly we praise his flat belly, his long,
well-muscled legs, and for hours each day
we admire his strength, agility, his grace
on the courts, his tennis whites bright
      against his wet brown skin –

    My wrecked body,
on its downhill journey, however meandering my course,
cannot fill your longing for your own body, climbing briskly,
inexhaustibly upward – a longing for the younger man
you never were —— and to press the weight of the world

up and off your shoulders, to lightly jog
before the years, tirelessly lapping yourself,
topping your personal best.

While I stand in the garden, a book forgotten in my hand,
gazing out over the rows of lupine and forget-me-nots,
you are passing on the road below
your hard well-muscled legs
running,
running.

Twenty Minutes Ahead of the Fire

The children first, of course. The animals.
Then what? Your black leather jacket?
The Persian rug? My book, your letters,
the photo albums, computers, all the discs,
the paintings, children's scrapbooks,
memories, metal boxes, locks, lamps,
Frye boots, leather bags, ancestor bones,
bins, sins, regrets, home videos, proof
of happiness, joys, jobs well done,
half done, undone, undoings, ghosts, toys,
good riddances, second chances,
last chances, no chances, dances
in the living room by night
naked before the fire, you kneeling,
the wish, a thin wish, slim wish,
dish of spaghetti, gathered family,
wine, empty bottles, spilled wine,
the all mine, gun on the mantle if you
ever touch another, the new you,
suddenly trim, blue-shirted you,
blue bottles, jewelry, recipes, news,
baby pictures, money, all the money,
handmade fairy dolls, quilts,
the smoke is every- fucking
(gun on the mantle) where.

The Complaint of Noah's Wife

All my clothes have faded in the sea air,
the endless damp, the mold on everything,
not to mention the stench! My red dress
long since faded to pink, I want
the dry desert air, the crisp breath
of pine needles on the mountainside
in sunshine. I remember lying
beside him when he was mine,
when I was a sweet branch of spring
blossom in his arms, caught in the tangle
of his shining beard – before the flood,
before the supposed Visitation took him
by the balls and pushed him
onto this floating bowl of suffering.

Theories
after Cirque du Soleil

The wizard in the metallic green vest
silver shoes that curl at the toes
comes out pushing his marvelous machine
clearly assembled from spare parts
in multi-colors with rare horns and whistles.

His assistant, small and quick, rushes on,
a rubber chicken swinging from one fist,
in her other arm a huge puff of cotton candy.
The magician is pleased. He rubs his
hands together in elaborate eagerness
and together they climb up and feed
first the chicken, then the pink fluff,
into the blue bell of the magical machine.

The satisfied assistant hurries off stage
and the wizard thoughtfully turns the crank –
loud grinding noises, vague absent looks –
and then, suddenly, from chicken and spun sugar,
stars!

Red Irises

I choose peach pie, I choose the walk
in shaded places, the afternoon nap
with a drowsy book, the sprinklers hissing
on the undulating lawn; you choose
sex in the hammock, (kids in the TV room).

I choose digging alone in the garden,
the dog asleep in the shade. You choose
Wittgenstein, pot smoking, weight lifting.
You choose satin sheets, X movies,
remodeling the house, a new stereo.

I choose a pastel drawing of a brown hillside
in Marin, pale sky, green cedars, blue fog.
I choose you.
You choose thick oils erupting off the canvas:
red irises, thick leaves waving in a high wind.
You choose me.

Ask Me
(for Charles at 62)

This is a poem for you:
because you asked me
because the steely silver blade
of your truth telling defends me muddled
keeps me safe from the deep night
of my own scurrying confusion
slices my enemy   fear
and leaves it lying in the dust:
you so shining, you my silver knight.

Because you stand so solid,
take all odd and unaccountable assaults
from your wild-haired woman in the courtyard,
who sends you off to battle with rivers
of tears, with cold regard,
with furious pummeling and wild fight

because inside your armor of worldly might
I know your tender taking and giving of all
strange needs and fantasies and curiosities found
at the beach – because you asked me:

if you go out in your clown suit
and no one laughs, I will. If you tell me
now that all the deep blueness of you
that I love has gone green,
I will throw off this dress, wail,
shake my hair, even stamp my feet;
I will weep and demand you blue,
but finally I will lie down in green grass,
pull at it, tear, coax the color
into my skin, I will go greener than
anything living on the planet

to stand inside the circle of your knowing.
I will put my vanity back in the pot,
comb out my wild hair, because you asked me,
asked me,
        ask me,
                oh ask me again.

Getting Done

Painting white walls white,
clearing emails one by one:
clicking in, reading short funny messages
from friends, sending quick funny replies,
erase; reading requests for information,
sending information, erase; reading
rambling diatribes on water usage and New Age
fuzzy prayers for World Peace, erase.

This painting goes smoothly,
one smooth swath laid beside another,
all the sticky hand prints, gone;
heel marks, gone; tiny push-pin holes,
filled, gone white, check, erase.

Soon your whole day goes this way:
groceries, check; post office, check; erase;
lunch, check; nap, check; erase; walk dog, check;
spend time with husband, check; erase.

You're moving along behind your life
as fast as you can go – painting over
the mess you made the day before –
Thursday, check; summer, check; youth, check;
erase.

Autumn

A breeze comes up, the wind chime
jingles faintly down the decks, and the heat beast
shakes its heavy body, lumbers to its feet, lurches
away down the canyon, leaving us dizzy and light.

Soccer cleats appear on the kitchen floor,
jackets, sweatshirts are flung onto the chairs
and suddenly, we feel the earth turning
under our feet. Time, which had lain

so still, paralyzed under the thick belly
of summer, lifts its head,
sniffs the air for change, rises,
sets out toward the horizon.

This chapter will end,
and in a time and place we cannot see
we will hold the memories of this day,
roll them around in our dark pockets
like smooth stones from the river,
feel how they hold the heat.

Clearing the Land (Menopause)

Standing in twists of vinca like slender nylon ropes
I lift the rotting log, break it, or it breaks
under its own weight, black ants erupt
like lava as I pitch it over my head
down the ravine, a few ants drop lightly
into my hair, but my ankles pull up
against the tangled vines, I sway,
the sweat running down my sides
and between my itchy breasts while the fine dirt
prickles along my arms and the black
berry vines seem to rise up on their own
to reach out for my face, my set mouth.

My husband is sawing through a larger limb
dead across the road; I find my balance,
pull my foot loose, draw myself up and center
clean and righteous, *You are so!*
and all those children *Be still*
for God's sake. You are all so!

I give my old last name on the phone.
I say *May* when I mean *November.*
I can't introduce all my friends around the table.
I am so *angry...*
        There is
poison oak under my feet the vines are snagging.
I am the black thorny vine loaded with so many berries
shriveled and hard although we picked bucketsful
and devoured hundreds as we worked,
the sweet red juices staining our fingers
our soft and swollen lips.

Hot Flashes

Not pain but a blushing,
a deep engine chugging in the delicate body,
smoldering out through the skin,
an internal sauna
so that tiny drops pop through
and gloss the face, the throat,
the soft, hidden sides under the dress
sodden with slippery wet
sliding down – the hot hair lifted,
drenched, from the neck.

Rude hormones, like bad tenants,
are having yet another good-bye party
before they move away forever,
stealing the silver candlesticks from my hope chest
and the poster of Ho Chi Minh.

Every night they wake me from my deep sleep,
my dreams of the river flowing backwards up the mountain
away from the greedy sea —
to a crashing on the stairs,
drunken shouts, stupid hilarity
around the bonfire on the lawn
where the old furnishings,
the beautiful things my parents gave me
when I first moved in,
piece by piece, night after night,
go up in flames.

Randomness
after September 11, 2001

In those last few moments I slept
in a cottage by the sea, rocking
safely in the boat of our bodies,
slept while the man
walking to work smelled
cinnamon buns in a bakery,
resisted for his diet's sake, walked on
and then, at the very entrance to his building,
turned and went back, and so
was not there among his friends
on the ninety-third floor
when their bodies were incinerated
in a ball of flame brought to them
by a plane carrying the woman
who was tired of New York, wanted
suddenly to return home to her cottage
by the sea, changed her flights,
thought herself lucky to get
the last seat.

For Gabriel Catalfo 1983-1999

His parents' hands sit empty in their laps:
no soup to bring, I.V. to change,
hand to hold. No hand to hold.
His father, reading the Tibetan
Book of the Dead, held it sleeping, in his own,
felt the breath come, go,
then not come again.
Rousing the mother from her
exhausted tossing, they held him finally,
while the door to a back bedroom
swung open, and a spirit passed.

Rarely in that seven years had they held him –
in his growing maleness, he fought them off,
their tears, their embraces a threat
to his strength of purpose: to see it through.

Only once, after the experimental drug,
when his shudders grew so violent,
the doctor asked his dad
to lie down there in the hospital bed,
hold him and share with Gabriel his own body heat:
a last and only chance to give him
something he could use.

Now it is done and in this moment they rest,
before time moves forward,
the long immovable anguish rushes in
and they take up the book
and begin to write how life will go on.

In this hushed hour may they fall back
against their pillows and partake
of peace for, as at his birth,
they have been mindful,
wholly present in the hours of his passing
both into and out of their lives, our lives,
this world.

Now again we, the blurry watchers
around the circle of their drama,
outside the fire's light, hurry in with warm blankets,
whispered words, longing to be of service,
some hoping to touch the hems of their gowns,
some crushing our own sons fiercely to our hearts,
all in awe that someone has come and gone,
that they, and hence we, had the ordinary
and the magnificent honor
of being guided by Gabriel.

The Recital

The mother sits at the piano
she has been playing all her life.
Her dress is pale yellow, neat and unobtrusive.
In front her daughter in a red taffeta dress
hair gleaming, velvet ribbon, plays a shining flute,
her new socks so white they glow.

As the flute notes rise, clear but uncertain, one by one
and then in smatters, the mother's fingers pause,
leap, pause again. Her head turned, her neck aching
toward the child, her entire attention arcs from her eyes
to her daughter's face, absorbing her intentions just as they
form, anticipating a falter, a flurry, a perfect passage.

And the piano never fails.
The girl stares out the window,
her face a mask of concentrated tension
as erratic clusters of notes arise gleaming,
cushioned in their luminous backing,
the silk lining beneath the diamond tiara,
each tentative passage shaped, released
into the room whole and lovely.

We are permitted to share
in their perfect connection.
And our tears are for this:
how hard-won it is
and a little for the passing
of the mother's music.

The Door

The woman wakes. In the dim light,
her husband, a tall shadow, fumbles in the dark
at the closet door. His eyes are bandaged.
He needs the bathroom.
"What are you looking for?" she asks.
Suddenly he is the child she never knew
standing barefoot in blue pajamas
turning solemnly toward her, his voice
soft, his answer timid, asking –
"I'm looking for the door?"
"To your right," she says, her heart
leaping to embrace him, to gather him up,
keep him safe.

          She remembers a moment
years ago, their little son, learning to walk,
falling forward on the basketball court,
his older brother, loping by, lifting him up
by the scruff of his neck in one deft maneuver
and standing him on his feet.

          She reaches for the covers but
he has found the door
and is gone.

The Mothers Speak: What We Want

We drive our kids to soccer in mini-vans
with power windows or to dance class
in little cars that rattle and rust.
We sing with them or to them
on the highway up the mountain,
Carol King, James Taylor on the tape,
or with no kids in the car, just our best friends,
on the way to some women's event, everybody speaks
at once, laughing, or we drive silently with one friend
who cries in the car
because of what she wants.

She wants her girl to get some special help
because she's slow in school. She wants
someone to see that girl's sweetness
behind the sullen mouth. And your friend
who does your hair, she wants her boy
to make some friends, to eat better,
and your friend next door — she wants
her girls to be good at math the way
she never could. The mom
at the soccer game confides
she wants to yell less,
listen better.

        The camera pulls back
and all the mothers are talking, crying,
holding each other in cars and kitchens,
laughing on the mountainside.
We want our girls to play a sport,
our boys to dance. We want

our kids to make a joke and grin,
have gardens, sleep soundly
and wake up in a safe house.

We want our girls "to speak their minds
even if their voices shake," to look
in the mirror and see themselves,
whatever their size and shape,
through our eyes, how beautiful they are,
the way their souls shine through.

We want our boys to slip through a peaceful window
in history, where no one dresses them in olive green,
shouts in their faces, sends them off
to have their lovely bodies torn and ruined;
we want our sons to grow up, read Thoreau,
play football in the dusky grass, toss their babies
in small bursts of joy.

We want to pause in the clarity of this bright day
and find our place, how each of us
is our own brave mother's child, each a link to the children
who hold our hope in their familiar hands,
to stand together on this mountainside
and know we have the power
by adding one or two or three good humans to the pot
to change the world.

Your Face

Well, I been afraid of changin'
'cause I built my life around you.

Stevie Nicks

Midlife

When enough river has poured through me
and I am clean, smooth and hollow,
I hug the winding ribbon home,
the tired dog beside me,
the leaves, green and gold, massed
beside the road in a blur of promise.

> We are descending our lives, yes,
> but slowly, as slowly, really, as we came up,
> long pauses for rest on the flat spots.
> Perhaps the going down will take as long
> as the coming up.

An empty vessel now, I come from the car
and the kids pour into me, their clear voices tossing,
their sweatshirts, blue and pink and green, gyrating.
They fill me with their jumble and clang,
their raucous wishes and their dreamy cries.

Meanwhile, down 49, impervious,
the Yuba River spills over the Sierra to the sea
like an endless dream: all night voices
murmuring as they slip, they slip away.

Blue Whales

Blue whales are out there somewhere,
six thousand of the hundreds of thousands
who once roamed the planet's seas.
Now separated from each other
by thousands of miles, they moan their loneliness
four octaves below middle C, so low, so slow,
we humans cannot even hear. But on our ocean liners
and in our lighthouse kitchens, the cutlery jangles on the table,
the glass pane vibrates in its frame, and we know
something nearby is crying out for love.
Two thousand miles away, they can be heard
and answered, the loudest sound made by a living thing,
and we don't know what it says, but only that,
speeded up ten times, what we hear is a long, blue,
unearthly note, a gurgle so deep
we slip down into our own lostness,
grateful that they are carrying for us
something bigger than we could hold.

You, You Mean

Working the shiny skeins of hair
into smooth golden braids down to her waist,
I ask companionably whether the tooth fairy
brought anything interesting last night.
In a flat voice she says, *You, you mean.*

And then we are caught up in the storm
of school bound forces
as she rushes out to feed the cats,
the others swarm in to fill the void,
and the Susan B. Anthony dollar shines
in its own secret mystery under her pink flannel pillow.

All day the dollar shines behind my eyes,
the magic of it, the pink glittered wings of the fairy
who slipped it in by night,
made off with her second molar
in a purple velvet bag.

At the end of yoga class
we lie flat in the dark, *savasana.*
The teacher says, *Experience the joy of all you have.*
And the fairy flits across the dark bank
of the moonlit river of my heart
on her way to another, younger child.

After Snorkeling at Molokini Crater
(with Katy, age 12)

In the light world our arms and faces
freckle in the sun, our eyes scan the horizon
for boats, the illusion of the visible world
spread before us on an aqua rippled plate
while below the shiny, opaque surface of the water,
our invisible lower halves roam in the dark,
bare legs slicing forward, pushing aside
the weight of water to reach the next unseen
niche, gliding past the poison fish, the pointed rock.

Chatting, we paddle our legs beneath us.
Naked limbs languorous, cycling slowly,
we are unaware that we have moved out
of the crater, over the steep edge of the world.
If we tried, we could not see the bottom now.
Cavern walls rise steeply and fall beneath us, teaming
with mysterious creatures, pink and blue and orange,
who live here. We are strangers.
The water's surface is dark, impenetrable.

Oblivious of the sheer drop, the sharks beyond the rim,
we splash, smile, holding the sun of the known world
in our eyes, and, as though I can keep you safe,
you hold my hand.

Being Left Alone in the Center of Things

See, honey, how your long bones lengthen,
how your flat hip sends the sap
down through the marrow to the square knob of knee –
That's your daddy's leg bone:
he planted the notes for that bone
deep inside me on the leather couch
while your brothers dreamt their own dreams
and the stars whistled a clear October tune
over the Berkeley hills.

See when he walks by on his way to mow the lawn
in his baggy shorts, how his heavy bone drops
just so.

      And see how your mouth turns down at the corners
making you look stern when you're only thinking
of which dress to wear tomorrow
or rotating a math equation in your mind.
That's Grandma's mouth, carried in the secret program of an
egg that waited in my left ovary for forty years
in case there was a chance to send you rolling down
the dark blood tunnel and push you,
huge and sleepy, out into my waiting arms.

Hold my hand so I don't feel this terrible lightness,
so I remember how you are the link beyond me
in this long strong chain in which I stand,
past the center of my life,
childishly clutching the link behind.

Grandma talks to her invisible long-dead father
all day behind the thin walls, worried neighbors.
Her stern-looking mouth, telling me this, goes slack

with surprise and sorrow. She is letting go of me
like a forgotten balloon from the hand of a distracted child.
She wanders uncertainly down a long road,
her eyes fixed on a distant point I cannot see
but feel as fear.

I am left here bobbing and floating,
unattached to the earth, looking back for her,
looking forward for you, my Long Tall Sally.
I am beginning to drift. Take hold of the string,
my perfect rose, my reason, my serious girl child:
take my hand.

Making Dinner
(For Katy, Age 11, newly diagnosed)

She lifts her shirt, wedges it between her elbow and her smooth
chest, scrutinizes her belly for a brown space
between lavender and yellow bruises.
Long-bone fingers
that pluck her small harp quick and light

move slowly from spot to spot
fleshing out pain and sorrow
for the sweetness of her sweet child's
unprotected underside, soft.
Two fingers pinch the little flap
while the other hand brings the plastic cylinder
designed to hide the needle she has filled with insulin
up against the skin. Deep breath.
Slow deep breath, and the click.

Setting the table, stirring the eggs,
I do not feel the sharp hurt, the slow ache
as she presses the plunger, slowly, one centimeter,
rest, one centimeter, rest,
the kind of child who takes her Band-Aid off
one filament of sticky at a time.

I do not feel the tender swellings
of her dozens of tiny wounds
and I must not weep.
I serve the eggs.

Things You Never
Thought You Could Do

Say you went to the refrigerator in your socks
and found, beside the yellow bowl of lime Jello and bananas,
two small vials of insulin: Humalog
for the fever of sandwiches and cake
and Ultralente for the long nights.

Say you went to wake your daughter,
the one with dreamy doe eyes,
who drifts into and out of days
on an aimless excursion
taken up by the beauty of every leaf
and who has yet to fasten her silver spirit
to a forward-moving engine.

Say you found her on the bathroom floor
half naked, wedged between the tub and toilet
her long arms twitching
small animal noises bubbling from her mouth.

Would you weep?
Would you step back in shock
and look away? Wait for someone
who knew what to do to appear,
an EMT, a specialist, your mother?

No, you would not.
You would step forward and pull her up into your arms.
You would send one of the children for her blue denim bag
from the kitchen counter, rub the tube of glucose
gel into her gums.
In a loud, firm voice you would tell her *Swallow.*
Swallow. And you would not relent.

If she lay heavily against your breast,
her teeth locked against your fingers,
you would lay her easily on the white bath mat
and turn to the cloth bag for the long red case
the emergency syringe you have studied but
never used.

Standing at the mirror, you would fill the syringe with glucagon,
your freckled hands shaking hard out over the sink.
You would turn back to her long flank, brown with summer
    swimming,
kneel down and slide the needle quick before you could think
into the muscle, ease the plunger down.
Then you would sit down on the floor, pull her
into your lap, and wait.

Waiting, would you croon her name,
rock her, sing her baby songs, caress the lank hair
back from her empty face?

And later, after her lost-looking eyes,
the mysteries of the words *chew, cracker, table*,
the nausea, vomiting, the stepping into the shower beside her
to help her remember how to wash her hair,
would you sit in the front seat of your best friend's car
clutch your bottled water and sob?

Say after slipping into her room every night
to stick her fingers, check her blood sugar,
you lay awake for hours
refiguring her carb-to-insulin ratios.
In the mornings, watching her laugh,
would you recalculate the value of every hour?

Spanish Dancer with Diabetes
(to the music of "Barcelona Nights")

Little long-legged girl in black tights,
long-stemmed white daisy
slipped from your vase and skipping,
sunny head spinning, petal hair flying

Spanish music, your clapping castanets,
I smell the sweet hay of your hair.
You circle past me in the kitchen
and I grab you quick, feel your bony ribs,
flat white belly; the heat of you,
the joy, flash in my hands.

I can spin, I can still spin:
light, dark, light, dark, light!

The Conversation

On the plane to Cleveland, across the aisle
my daughter gives herself a shot,
learning to perform this ritual in public places.
The woman beside me
tells me sympathetically about her friend
whose two children both died of diabetes,
long, hopeless deaths of kidney failure,
blindness, amputated feet.

I slide to the floor sobbing,
my hands to my face,
my heart leaping against my ribs.

Or no. I turn and slap her hard.
Her face registers honest amazement;
her eyes fill with tears.

Well, no. I look to make sure my daughter didn't hear.
I excuse myself politely, walk back to the restroom.
I stand there a long time
shaking.

The Long Night

The mother and daughter hike Yosemite.
As they rest below Sierra Point, a passing hiker
tells them about the avalanche of '95, points above
to where the lip of granite at the top
sank away into the valley, tells how the wind
from the collision with the floor tore up
trees, threw them, crushing someone
who had taken refuge under the refreshment
stand.

      When they reach the high ledges
the mother suddenly feels how she might
lose her balance, fall backward
into the valley below, how the wind
of her landing would barely stir the dust.

At night the mother sleeps on a cot
in a canvas cabin, anchored to the earth
by the village of voices and footsteps –
her daughter beside her, wrapped in a light
blue sleeping bag on the other cot –
the cocoon in which she is becoming
a woman.

The mother dreams
there is a half-eaten apple
pressed against her vagina
between her closed legs.
She lies naked on her back,
unspeakably beautiful,
and men like horses
are grazing nearby
hungry for apples.

She touches herself
under a tent of blankets
silently so as not to wake
her daughter, deep
in her whorl of quilts.
She shudders, her hand pressed
hard to the button,
the apple core.

Now the mother dreams she has traded bodies
with a beautiful friend, young, thin,
elfin, and that in this body she can fly.
Her wings glitter faintly, pink and green.
She flies up a Cinderella stairway
into a huge hall where her friends
are gathered for a feast, circles over
their heads, looks down at her beautiful friend
and sees
        that after all there has been no trade,
that in her own worn body
she can fly!

        In the mother's next dream
she stands with her daughter on top of a cliff, feels a trembling,
a crumbling of the earth under their hiking boots.
Turning, they grab hands, run away from the edge,
the girl a stride ahead, and as they pause to look back
a crack opens between them. The rim is splitting off,
sinking, and the mother is going down.
She feels her daughter's intention to hold on, to save her,
and, seeing how the girl will be pulled down by her weight,
she yanks her hand free. Standing on the falling crust of earth,

she looks up at her beautiful daughter
who now, like a child, cries down to her *Mama*,
her face wet, contorted with anguish, and the mother
wakes, crushed with the sorrow
of lost mothers.

This Is Just To Say
(with a wave to William Carlos Williams)

Thank you for the peach pie
red gold, gooey, thick and crusty:
peaches carried heaped in a basket
up the hill from the tree we planted
seven years ago, watched over,
pruned, debugged, (harvested
one rock of a peach that first year)
and now its branches bent to the ground
on the uphill side, their burden of fuzzy
softening fruit almost more joy
than they can bear.
                         You rolled the dough
while I peeled fruit into a pail
my hands deep in the juice and pulp
my mouth smeared where I sucked
my fingers, my hair sticky on my forehead,
tiny fruit flies buzzing in the kitchen.

I helped you lift the flat crust with spatulas
and we laid it safely in the pan. You spiced
the golden bowl with cinnamon and other secrets,
crisscrossed the top with lattice crust,
and this morning, you gone off to school,
I cut a piece and served it on a small blue plate
with milk in a blue cup.
                        I ate it slowly,
noticing every bite, watching the grasses move
as the breeze swept across the distant hills.

I've left the rest for you, sweet baker girl.
I'll be gone a few days,
but I'll be thinking of you
eating peach pie.

Nate's Question

Oh you. You were a great idea we had
one warm June afternoon after Ross left
and we had drunk three glasses of white wine
in the garden and eaten all the yellow and orange cheeses
and Ritz crackers and even the Saltines,
and Ben was at his dad's and Caleb was at his mom's
and we said, *Let's not wait for the final papers.*
Let's not wait anymore; I don't want to wait,
he said, and I said, *I can't wait anymore,*
and we started toward the living room
and I was wearing my high heels that make
my calf muscles long and light and my new
peach silk come-hither thing and we never
made it past the front hall, where
we rolled and moaned and entered once and for all
deeply and permanently into each other's lives.

And on vacation in Maui, where you were *supposed* to begin,
I was sinking and rising on my belly's random tides
and he said, *Not yet. I wanted to spend a long time trying.*
But I didn't jump off the waterfall with the boys.
I laid in the sun, my flat belly browning and cooking
and he sat down beside me with a large pink plumeria
for my belly button.

                In the hospital, he gave me
a scribbled note on a scrap of paper that said,
Thank you. He's just what I wanted.

When you were three we left you home.
Lying on a beach in Kuai, drifting together toward sleep,

I said idly, *If you had to spend the rest of your life
on an island with only one person, and it couldn't be me,
who would you choose?* thinking Ghandi, Wittgenstein, Jefferson ...
Without hesitation, he said your name.
So you. You're the present we paid for in advance
and will still be loving a long time after.

The Wrestling Tournament

On the blue mat
a fat boy, an ugly boy,
some mother's son, but enemy
to me, rushes my son,
grabs him, flips him onto
his lean brown back
rubbed only last night
by my tired hands,
holds him down,
mean, persistent, strong
fingers biting into sweet skin,
he leans his hideous bulk,
my boy arching,
the cords of his neck taut
and straining, his shoulders
stretched above the mat,
inches away, and is he slowly
sinking, going down in despair,
defeat? My body feels the strain,
leans for him, yearns
to run out there,
grab that bully kid,
fling him against the wall,
run him through with my shining
sword, cradle my furious, (ungrateful)
warrior. But the barbarians
are at the gates and all is lost —
he's pinned.

After hours of waiting in dank corners,
fighting to breathe 20 years of sweat-ground,
rubber-mat fumes, slipping outside gratefully,
standing in the drizzle on the brown school yard,

idly munching nachos and chemical cheese,
at last: next match.

This new opponent's wiry:
flushed, innocent expression,
but I am wary, cannot
sympathize. He circles my boy
crouching, hands hanging,
swinging out like clubs,
hoping to grab sturdy legs
also circling, tense and expectant,
both of them *thinking* –
it's that kind of match –
going over the next potential
move – chess, with bodies,
and very fast – my boy lunges in,
pulls a spindly leg out and under,
rolls over him, his chin mashed
into the mat, leans his weight
hard into the enemy's bony chest,
20 seconds, 30, he presses down
calling on gravity for all it can add,
the red-cheeked boy flailing,
straining mutely to keep one
shoulder off the mat, he rolls one
eye back to see how far he has to go,
while I, forgive me, think *Get him
Get him*, what would be,
in another time and place,
Kill him, and the boy is down,
my good boy glazed with sweat,
fierce and not smiling,
his sword arm aloft
in victory.

Are You Mine?
(for Nate at 13)

Light as a bug, you hopped up into my arms,
wrapped your legs around my waist
and burrowed into me, the scent of me you loved.
(You kept the lipstick that I threw away
so you could smell me when I'm gone …)

You climbed over me, crawled on and under me
on sofas, rugs, beds, with great gigglings –
my body yours, your body mine.

And now you shout at me to stop talking
while you are watching TV,
your face cold with anger.
You have private phone calls,
and my hands drop away from your silky hair.
We look away.

I knew you couldn't stay.
But I have been adored,
and my life's the less
for your going.

For Nate, Wanting Desperately to Grow

Nathan's wishes and desires
keep him awake all night
with their constant bickering:
wait, love and be funny/
rush forward, fight and be king.

His body bunches for its final assault
on adulthood. His adrenaline pumped
for the attack, he waits
and waits
and waits
for the call to battle,
for the last hormonal soldier to show up
running, his shoe laces dragging,
swelling the ranks to the necessary volume
to thunder forth at last
up the ladders and over the walls,
flooding into the fortress –
a giant of a man,
easily wielding a heavy sword,
causing conquered maidens to swoon
both at his power and his obvious wit,
and willing, finally, to show compassion
to those who ridiculed him while he waited,
calling him coward or *Shorty*,
assigning them lives of hard labor
but letting them live.

Soon he will hardly remember the waiting time.
His new life will absorb him completely
and he will study to be a good and just king.
His natural sense of rightness will take him far,

his reasonableness in the face of fools,
his love of music and intelligent naked women
for whom he will know how, if necessary,
to wait.

The Dance Show

All the yellow flowers open.
Petals lift and swirl
around slim sturdy legs,
the stage afloat with girls
under the golden lights
as they perform their last dance,
last night, last show
before flying away on the college breeze,
the New York breeze,
the marriage/baby wind at their backs.

In my memory Caitlin sits on a wall
other kids screaming around her,
dreamy faced and lost in a book.
But now, in red and black,
the girls vamp across the stage,
hips circling in the eternal summons,
and I see how for Caitlin, front and center,
this is as natural as sleeping and waking
(while for Sara, in the back,
who lives in her meticulous brain,
it is still a foreign language).

In the next dance Stephanie, dressed as a rose,
steps delicately on green stems, slim and precise,
fragile arms lifting up out of the red-petal
bodice as she commands her space,
quick small body moving through air.
No sign now of the blank despair, the lost girl
we have been fearing for. Here is a swan,
at home on her pond of music.

And Jessica, halo of orange hair, awkward as a fawn
only last week, dips now and spins firmly
in her yellow dress, a thing of the past
her laughter in my kitchen,
her voice woven among the others in song:

I am beautiful, in every single way.
Words can't bring me down.
Don't you bring me down today.

All the girls circling, petals fluttering,
open further now, their faces turn up
to the lights, hair pulled back
so that each shining face is revealed in its trust,
its hope, its tentative confidence.

And we who have watched over these girls,
stand fixed, tears in our eyes,
and applaud.

The Journey
(for Nate)

Packing his bag
the boy spent years.
Knowing he needed to travel light
he saved in tiny parcels only the end products
distilled from all the words
he'd heard, those meant for him
and those overheard in other rooms.
He collected, sorted and analyzed
the successes and failures of others,
jokes that were or were not funny, and why.
He saved *What love feels like*
and *Don't step on the heater with bare feet.*
He saved *Winning* and discarded
Slow down and *Don't try so hard.*

There came a moment
when they knew his pack was almost full.
The information pockets bulged
and so, in the last few weeks,
they only tucked in little extras:
Back scratching and *Companionable silence in the car*,
hoping that when the time came
it would be enough.

Justice

In my town on a street of plain houses
I drive up behind two police cars
double parked,
                cops climbing out,
ambling across the lawn as the front door
opens,
          a young girl steps out, meets them
on the steps.
              I slow to pass the cars
as a young man the age of my son,
clean cut, open collar,
                    steps out behind her,
she speaking now to the cops,
                and then
he steps forward, his wrists
extended so that I see, with shock,
the silver handcuffs glitter in the huge hands
of the cop, taking them off his belt,
                    and,
as my car eases past in the street,

the boy looks up, meets my eyes briefly,

and in that instant I receive his fear,
huge and almost overpowering,
but also his courage, his resolution
as he presents himself,
                  now past wishing to god
he hadn't done last night whatever thing he did,
past the long night talking with the girl over coffee,
phone calls to her uncle for advice,

                              past the embarrassment
of childish tears, runny nose,
                    the blind interval
in the back bedroom,
her comforting body one last time.

I see, in that instant, his readiness now
to move forward into the system of strangers,
hard lights, cold hands, alien clothing,

where he will be made to suffer
whatever justice is to come.

THE LESSON
(for Ben)
Meat bees like grease, sweat, meat, flesh. They're carnivores.

How many bees was it?
Was it a whole hive
or an angry threesome
drawn to your sweaty neck,
your red T-shirt pressing
them into your armpits
the small of your long sticky back?

Screaming you came
scrambling up over the fence
faster than you've ever climbed.
I ran toward you, my hands out,
to stop whatever was hurting you.

Where were all the bees?
The red shirt, yanked up over your head,
dropped one into your hair.
Your father flapped one away with the shirt
while I flicked another from your cheek.

Red noise filled the yard
echoed down the hill through the live oaks.
Was I screaming?

Weeping quietly at last, you whisper:
*I held still when the first one came
so I wouldn't scare him.
Why did he sting me anyway?*

Riding with Ben, 19

Ben, brooding giant, drives upright
staring silently at the straight road,
his great hands clutching the wheel,
rock music speaking for him, loud and brave,
beating on the metal truck, bass notes
assaulting its hollow frame, louder than noise,
vibrating around and through us, and I,
beside him, his silent human captive,
squeezed in the fist of sound,
hold very still, play dead,
propelled, in a pulsing silver bullet,
down Highway 49.

Your Face
(for Ben at 17)

I see the day is turning you in grace.
Both of you come dancing into spring,
the light, the darkness, split across your face.

A brief caress in lieu of an embrace,
a secret listen at the door to hear you sing,
I hear the day is turning you in grace.

Standing in doorways arguing your case –
we learn the dark of love, the slap, the sting.
The light, the darkness split across your face.

Slammed in your room, you brood in your disgrace,
crow of remorse stretching a crippled wing,
but still the day is turning you to grace.

Long is the time though furious the pace
waiting for life beyond this silent aching,
the light, the darkness, split across your face.

A shadow man is standing in your place.
This is the gift we knew that time would bring.
I see the day is turning you in grace;
the dark, the lightness, spill across your face.

What the Mind Wants

Barn burned down. Now I can
see the moon.

Basho

An Aging Woman
(with gratitude to Yeats' Sailing to Byzantium*)*

This is no country for old women, the young,
fragrant and tight skinned, stalking about
in high heels and tiny shirts, flat bare bellies,
tossing their long thick hair. Their pains
are short, intense and legitimized in every film,
novel, the pains of love and loss, of loneliness,
the pains of not getting what you want when you want it.

There is no celebration of the sorrows
that are neither glamorous nor subject to cure,
the sorrow of things that are ending and will never
be again. That the sweetness goes out of the bite,
the sharpness from the needle, the ecstasy from the peak,
even after so long and arduous a climb,
is a secret sensibly kept from the young
as protection from the knowledge of aging women
stumbling lost in a sea of half impressions,
near experiences, bugs that buzz by, or a flock of geese,
the murmured words *You look so lovely*
possibly coming from the TV set.

          And yet
someone should take them by the arm
and say how it will all disappear, how they should
run naked through the streets in their beautiful skins,
dance all night, speak their minds, live on the street, eat spicy food,
wear any damn thing they please, adore their wits,
their fabulous tongues, the full list of words to choose from
for any occasion, their hairless upper lips, perky breasts,
their smooth and spotless hands.

             An aging woman is an invisible thing:
she passes on the street unseen, unflirted with, unwhistled at,
her ass unspeculated on, and yet not ancient enough
to be offered a seat on the bus or guided across in traffic.
Young men, straightening their ties and gazing
past her shoulders, inquire after her *teaching, is it?* and
young women at parties leap away as though confusion
were contagious, as though invisibility spreads.

From women's bodies, the juices are licked away.
Hair flat and thin, the plump fruits of the vagina, thin and dry,
must, like rusted machinery, be oiled for a smooth run.
Release seems to be happening somewhere else,
somewhere nearby, and finally they offer their bodies up
as a gift only, or remembering moonlight and the music of Sade,
and in the longing to, as before, be loved.

For this creature that contains them,
this dying animal to which their hearts are fastened,
was their ticket to all life's joys, and now,
between passion and the eventual end,
what will they be?

Waiting to Be a Grandmother
(for Beth)

Hundreds of miles from here
she lies laboring
groggy and weak
from three hours of pushing
against the fuzzy shapeless thing
that will not come.
Somewhere down there
a baby waits, while a muffled train
roars against her backbone
wailing its need to pass.

My son's voice on his cell phone,
ebullient and confident at nine this morning,
sounds strained and exhausted at three.
The rain moves up the canyon,
hovers black on the hillside.

Within this daughter-in-law,
secret as an uncut book,
closed eyes, red lipstick scarred mouth,
the tenderest girl calls out for drugs,
some help for the baby riding on choppy seas,
a lone voyager in a solid boat,
heavy fog.

Come, rain.
Let this child be given.
Let this girl fall back in warm blankets
with no memory of pain.
Let time speed and this brave job be done,
well done.
Come, rain.

Olivia for a Minute

Often a toddler in ruffled baby clothes
I'd purchased at Costco in a fit of joy,
she was sometimes a little girl, brown bangs,
reading on the porch, smart, serious,
like her grandfather before her,

occasionally a long-legged
girl sewing quilts for my lap,
wheeling me around in my dotage,
fondly bantering with Grandma,
white-haired and ancient, but still
in full possession of my wits.

Email from my son:
"Tests are good.
Baby's fine.
It's a boy."

I lift my face to the window over my desk.
The California oak leaves, lush and green,
wave and ripple in the breeze.
Among them an infant with tiny wings,
grins as she ascends between branches,
sails off into puffs of cloud; Olivia
disappears.

Belly

Why do I malign you ruefully
in locker rooms or among friends
speak disparagingly of your unwillingness
to be exercised or dieted away?
Why hide you, fold hands over you,
walk naked with one hand before you,
screen you from the lover's eyes,
protect him from your droop,
your fold, your lumpy knolls?
Though we both apologize, saying how
you've been a good belly, taken
your share of reproductive knocks,
been required to stretch well beyond
the usual call of maternal duty,
why do we shun you? We appreciate you,
but our fingers never graze you, and
though the entire surface of my body
be polished till it gleams under his hands,
you lie untouched, untouchable,
your sloppiness an embarrassment,
my body's beauty all undone.

In the dark, spread out
full length, we press you to him,
and the heat at his center leaches
inward, spreads, and you, my belly, take,
if not forgiveness, comfort.

Wailing

I hiked down the steep rocky path
to the river, where someone
had impossibly hauled wood
for a small house, or shack really,
now deserted, and I climbed
over boulders in the sand,
finally reached the water
high and rushing in spring flood,
shinnied up and sat
on a smooth edge in the sun.
My German shepherd scrabbled below me,
lying down in the cold current,
lapping loudly and then subsiding
so the river was the only sound,
miles from anywhere, peace. And then
a loud unexpected noise,
a sob breaking out
into the open, another, the dog and I –
eyes meeting in mutual surprise –
What does it mean?
And then for a long time there was crying,
a wailing, the river accepting it all,
the whole weight of it
breaking up, shifting, lifting
out of my chest and returning
on the wind.

And when it was quiet again,
I climbed down onto the sand,
found a round stone for my pocket,
planted a tall tapered rock
pointing upward
standing
for my intention.

Laguna Beach

Just into our second Margarita we begin
our annual State of the Marriage exploration.
We have come here for this,
where the surf crashes around our bed upstairs
and down here in the restaurant, surrounded by strangers,
we are finally alone.

So little has changed since our last review,
we fumble in the dark for the invisible corners of words…
reaching back into the closet of recent memory
trying to discover that once most obvious of information:
how we feel.

Look, we say. *These mismatched socks, that outgrown jersey,
some snapshots, cracked and bent but still recognizable.*
Shall we pitch them overboard? We look them over,
exchange memories, come to find them dear.
We put them back. Nothing tells us anything we haven't learned
in five thousand days in a small boat.

The truth is, this boat is seamless and steady as she goes.
It takes on very little water, though we love this annual bailing.
And mainly we remember
that what sometimes seems so unwieldy,
so slow and awkward to maneuver,
an ocean liner under full power,
is still this small craft, and both of us rowing.

The First Creature

At first this bag of skin,
soft as if powdered with flour
and filled with bones,
lolls about shapelessly, shifting under your hands:
you solid, you large and also directionless.
There is a sea smell
neither sweet nor clean
but real, and older than we are,
holding us in its thick slow thrall.
I begin somewhere in the dark
to sense a plan,
the winds shifting till a clear direction's felt.
Your nipples begin to harden and lift under my hands.
Your whole body points toward a clear intention
and, rising up out of the mud,
I become a creature with a purpose:
to drive the matter home,
to settle the hard beating of you
into the soft socket,
complete the circuit,
lay the paddles to its chest
and jump the sleeping heart
of the new beast,
every window in the house
suddenly alight
as its eyes fly open,
its bellows echo
in a brand new world.

Practice

Practice piano. Practice patience.
And you know what practice makes.
At making love you have to practice for years
until one day you know you've got it right: a perfect 10,
your form simple and fluid, the harmony of your movement
from one mood to the next flawless,
and boy, can you two dance
to that unmistakable rhythm!

But will we be too old? Will spontaneity suffer?
Ask the Olympic diver — when he leaves that platform,
opens cleanly like a switchblade,
slices the air before us in triumph –
whether he suffers from having tried this dive
a thousand times in a single summer.
If he crumpled and hit like a stone,
that would be spontaneous:
                              a heart attack,
a pregnant child, a broken water main under your house –
these are spontaneity at its finest.

                              No, I want
to lie back slathered in fresh sweat
and recognize everything: your citric tang,
the soft bristly places, exactly how and when and where
to move my lips – every hungry action
finding its succulent round reaction. I like
the two of us heaped in our regular way
among the pillows and books – the only small change

being the books: their titles and colors,
the way their plots all come together at the end –
the word pictures that we draw from them, weave and braid
carefully into each other's dreams,
practicing storytelling, practicing listening.
We're getting ready for the final competition,
the really big event!

A Dying Planet

"If the fire at the heart of the earth were to go out, what would happen?"

As the tiny fire that propelled me toward you
in the long nights of our shared memory,
combusted into astonishing shades of orange
and iridescent green and lavender,
smoldered beneath the roll and crash
of the oceans that tossed and cradled us,
burned quietly below the land masses
of our daily lives, sustained us through car pools,
business trips, bad movies, three meals a day
as that tiny fire at the core began to cool,
we stoked frantically, bought lingerie, took
little blue pills, watched dirty movies.

We dropped ecstasy into the molten lava
at the lignite cracks, peered sadly into the steam
where the fire used to glow. And now, on this first
day of the new era, I see the fire is out. You are coming
cheerfully up the front walk, but the wild woman
has gone away. Leave flowers on the porch.

What will become of us? What kinds of matter,
what skills and workable philosophies,
have I wrapped around my core in a lifetime of creating
this dying planet? See how my trajectory begins to shift
as the molten liquid hardens, settles, and we circle
each other wobbling, seeking in the vast dark
some natural new orbit.

At Kona

In the lava tube
there is no room to stand.
I hunker down like a toad in the dark
move my feet awkwardly forward
toward the sphere of light
guiding me out to the sea.

I long to fall to my knees and crawl
so bent and hobbled am I
but the stalactites pierce my shoes,
poke and turn my ankles.

Our children scream and squeal
swinging along like apes toward the sun.
Their father enters last,
stoops forward and bends his knees strangely.
Drunken bear, he bumps along
staggering, his damaged eyes almost blind
in the dark, and as the ceiling lowers
he begins to reel off to the sides.
He cannot see the lava peaks pointing out
and down at him. His head cracks
against the ceiling, and again.

He throws up his arms, crouches lower.
The children are stunned. They rush back
to guide him, their serious all-knowing leader
now careening about in the dark.
They touch his arms, call out
in suddenly adult voices
guiding him *to the left, now crouch,*
now raise up and look for the light.

Together we help him
until we stand upright, drenched in sweat
in the awesome mouth
where lava once poured itself into the sea
thirty feet below.

The boys look back at their family
standing safe and solid in the light.
They glance at the "No Diving" sign,
grin, turn toward the sea, and yelling, Tarzan-like,
leap off into the sky.

Snoring

Not like at the hostel
where the old man's snorts and gurgles
burst forth erratically, always preceded
by a brief silence for maximum
explosive effect, so that sleep
came to us in small increments
broken again and again by his desperate
gasps and bombastic ejaculations of air
until we all gave up sleep and lay
furious in the dark
considering pillows over his face,
almost anything for an hour of peace.

No, this snoring, rhythmic and reliable,
I have hitched my dreaming to for 20 years,
linked my own breath to a more powerful machine
and let myself be towed
through the mysterious sea of night
the way the boys on our street
used to catch the wind behind a fast car
down Franklin Blvd., their bikes
flying in its wake,

the way my brother and I, down to our last dollar,
drove the interstate home in winter,
our dad dying in his bed,
our VW Beetle rusted full of holes,
no heater, and packed in blankets,
winter hats and gloves, we'd find a safe pocket
of wind behind a massive cargo truck
and draft the long cold night
snow sparkling in our headlights
like magical, untouchable dreams
and sail safely home to morning.

What the Mind Wants

Blessed, I am listening to rain
in a window seat looking out on my garden,
my birdhouse on a stilt
standing alone in the grass.

My friend is explaining globalization.
I listen carefully to two sentences,
less carefully to a third, and my mind
turns aside to watch a cat passing,
returns too late for the next phrase,
veers off into the refuge
of the palpable, the immediate,
the thing small enough to be lifted,
the simple recipe, three artichokes.

The mind wants what it can remember:
his firm body in the heat beneath me,
the scents and colors of flowers, if not the names,
the weight of a large warm dog against my knees,
leaning, blue cups lined up on a shelf, clean.

The time for giving off big light
is ending. What light I shed now
is a bi-product of this quiet living,
and I no longer pause to admire it
in the mirror. What's left is absorption.

> Is this fog (as we fear in the night,
> the bile of panic rising into our throats)
> at the mouth of a long tunnel
> narrowing, darkening as it moves us
> into blackness?

Or should we remember (as we know
in safe light on a good day) this:
We are more than the sum of our memories
and information, more even than the quick
and funny, the taut and beautiful,
the fine-honed edge of passion,
the dream of future.

I want to spend my last years on a wide porch
looking out on a green garden, golden light, color,
rocking in a white wicker chair, sweet scents on the breeze,
familiar young people who love me, and whom I love,
though perhaps I cannot remember,
coming and going, stopping to speak, to smile,
and I will pat their soft hair,
amazed at the glow,
taking it all in
gratefully.

Author

Gail Rudd Entrekin teaches English and Creative Writing at Sierra College. Her previous poetry collections are *John Danced* (Berkeley Poets Workshop & Press, 1984) and *You Notice the Body* (Hip Pocket Press, 1998). Poetry editor of Hip Pocket Press since 2000, she edited the anthology *Sierra Songs & Descants: Poetry & Prose of the Sierra* in 2002. She lives in Nevada City, California, with her husband and the youngest of their five children.

Artist

Steve Solinsky is a fine art photographer whose work explores the emotion of color, and the power and mystery of common scenes revealed in new light. *"Chamber of Light"* was captured in a monastery in a small town in the Oaxaca Valley of Mexico. It's one of a series of Mexico images the photographer has made on numerous trips to the south. More of his work may be viewed at solinskyphoto.com.

www.ingramcontent.com/pod-product-compliance
Lightning Source LLC
Chambersburg PA
CBHW031207090426
42736CB00009B/815